Options for Wealth

Brian Archer, MPA

Options for Wealth, c. 2011, http://optionsforwealth.weebly.com, Brian.Archer.13@gmail.com

Introduction

This book is meant for someone without extensive investment knowledge or experience.

Or, this book is meant for someone frustrated with their own particular investment knowledge and experience and is looking for fresh ideas in order to create a simple, yet exciting, "hands-on" strategy for taking control of their investing.

This book is meant to cut straight to the chase in normal, easy to understand language with just enough explanation to be practical. However, I'll try to provide as much context and background as necessary. There are literally millions of written pages devoted to the background and context of this subject. Read as much background and history as you like – I'll try to give you just what you need.

Fortunes have been made and lost on a nearly daily basis since the New York Stock Exchange formally began over 200 years ago. And, while riding that financial roller coaster through it's peaks and valleys, we have been lifted out of our seats with joy over seemingly cosmic windfalls and punched in the gut with equally fateful and unexpected financial downturns. So …

Why do we invest?

Pretty simple – We invest so we can have more money. But more specifically, we invest so we can reach our personal goals.

These goals are different for everyone but they usually involve having more money and they all usually involve the same amount of daydreaming.

We could be talking about short-term goals like saving for a car or a vacation. For these goals, we squirrel money aside in places where we can retrieve it easily like a savings account, or in a shoe box in the closet.

We may be investing in order to achieve longer-term goals like retirement or college tuition for the kids.

Situations like these won't require you to retrieve your money quickly or for quite some time.

Either way, people will be investing to create a nest egg for short or long-term goals even if that goal is just to have your money keep pace with inflation.

One quick word of advice before we move on ...

Write your goals down !

Anywhere - On your notebook, on the bulletin board in the kitchen, on the back of a receipt which you can keep in your wallet.

"A goal is a dream with a deadline." - *Napoleon Hill*

I've talked to many people who want to retire someday but can't tell me (in any way) what that means to them. I have heard things like this:

"You know, just retire" or,

"I'll figure that out when I get there" or the best one,

"that depends on how much money I'll have."

My advice is to at least start with something tangible and quantifiable like being able to have enough to provide yourself the income you are making now. Then figure how big your nest egg has to be to pull this off. This will give you a realistic starting point from which to jump off.

"Your future is created by what you do today, not tomorrow" - *Robert Kiyosaki*

For example, let's say you are bringing home $3,000/month. If that's the amount you intend to also bring home each month in retirement, how big a pile of money will you need? A $6,000 pile would last probably two months. A $36,000 pile would probably last a little over a year.

Get the picture?

Will this goal be too much? Too little? Don't decide to decide when you get there. It'll be too late at that point and you'll just be disappointed because whatever you actually have saved will most likely be less than what you thought you'd have.

We'll save goal setting for another time. Ever heard of "analysis paralysis?" This is when some people get stuck in a goal-setting daydream they can't get out of. This paralysis leads to not starting the program. Not starting the program leads to depression which leads to another grand realization to "do something" a month from now which leads to more daydreaming...

Chapter 1
<u>An Investing Primer</u>

Casey Stengel coached the New York Yankees to ten American League pennants and seven World Series Championships while managing the club from 1949–1960. On the first day of spring training, every year, Casey would gather the entire team on the field and walk them as a group from position to position explaining what each position was expected to do during a ball game and it's role to helping the club win games.

Casey had a championship ring made for his big toe.

What is a stock market?

The New York Stock Exchange (NYSE) was the first and remains the largest of America's stock exchanges. Originated in New York City back in 1792, literally on a quiet portion of Wall St., twenty-four men would regularly gather on the sidewalk to trade stock shares for themselves and others. These early stockbrokers didn't have much to work with, there were only 5 publicly traded companies back then. These days, thousands of brokers trade in person and electronically the approximately 3,000 publicly traded companies on the NYSE floor.

The NASDAQ (National Association of Securities Dealers) was started in 1971 as the first electronic, or computer-based, stock exchange. The approximately 3,800 securities traded on this exchange are different from those traded on the NYSE. The NASDAQ has the reputation of being "tech" heavy and that's mostly true. The companies that trade on the NASDAQ span the same industries as the other exchanges around the world. But with this exchange being newer and more "tech savvy," and most business startups these days occurring in the tech sector, it stands to reason these companies would be attracted to the idea of being listed here. However, the NASDAQ is still only comprised of about 40% tech stocks. Not significantly more than other exchanges around the world.

Speaking of around the world. America may have had the first and maintains the biggest stock market, but it hasn't cornered the market on stock markets. Nearly every developed country in the world, (and some non-developed countries) from the United Kingdom to Papua New Guinea to Mongolia, has a stock exchange these days. Some of these exchanges have also developed indexes much like how the U.S. has indexes like the DJIA and the S&P. Here's a list of some of the major indexes and the foreign exchange it represents.

Index	Country
DAX	Germany
FTSE	England
Nikkei	Japan
AEX	Netherlands
TSX	Canada
Hang Seng	Hong Kong, China
Shanghai	China

Typical Types of investments

Stock. Stock is simply partial ownership of a publicly traded company. A company will issue a number of shares of stock in order to raise business capital. People who buy shares of stock are literally buying a very small portion of the company and are entitled to a portion of the company's profits (or losses).

These shares get traded in the stock markets and carry the value equal to what people are willing to pay for them. If investors see a stock as a valuable asset, the stock value may rise. Oppositely, if investors do not see a company's stock as a significant asset, the stock value may decrease. For this basic reason stocks are classified by many as "volatile" or "risky" investments as the price may fluctuate often and possibly to extremes.

Bond. When a company or municipality is looking to raise money for capital improvements, they will issue certificates called bonds. Bonds are usually issued with a face value or par value to represent the amount borrowed. The entity issuing the bond promises to pay interest to the bondholder based on a percentage of that face value. For example, you may hold a bond for company XYZ with a face value of $500. XYZ company agreed up front that interest would accrue at 5% per year until you cashed it back in. After one year this means you would get your $500 back plus a cool $25 for the effort. Pretty good money for a year of letting XYZ borrow $500. Or is it?

Mutual Fund. This is merely a collection of shares of stocks in a variety of companies. The idea here is that if you own stock in one company you're financial success depends on the performance of that one company.   By investing in several (or hundreds) companies you are reducing your financial risk because it is unlikely they will all go belly-up at the same time. Think of it like playing roulette. You could put all your money on black 13. The payout would be huge if it hits. But what is the realistic chance it will hit? Or, you could split your money several ways and play a variety of numbers. The payout wouldn't be as great if you hit but you've just increased your chances of winning by a factor of 4 or more.

Money Market. This is pretty close to just being a savings account. Most commonly a portion of your money is invested in Treasury Bills which may return between 0 and 2% on a yearly basis. The rest may literally be kept lying around in cash earning no interest. These funds are obviously highly liquid and are often used to hold your money ready because you might need it soon.   Such as for purchasing an anticipated investment.

Major Indices

Dow Jones Industrial Average (DJIA)

This is the most widely used of all the market indicators and is composed of the 30 largest and most actively traded industrial stocks. The companies that comprise the DJIA represent all the major business sectors such as communications, utilities, technical, pharmaceuticals, and retail. This average regularly tracks the stock productivity of these companies and is price-weighted and does not reflect a dollar for dollar tracking of the sum of all the stocks in the index. I've provided a list of all the stocks currently represented in the DJIA.

S&P 500

Standard & Poor's is a financial services firm that performs analysis and publishes research on investment securities like stocks and bonds. It maintains an index called the S&P 500 and is based on the prices of 500 large-cap American common stocks that trade on the New York Stock Exchange and the NASDAQ. These 500 stocks are selected by a committee and are intended to represent the 500 biggest and most influential American companies.

Russell 2000

This is an index comprising of the smallest 2,000 listings based on capitalization ("small cap" stocks). Some people feel this index is a better indicator of what "real America" is doing because it is not distorted by the largest trading companies, or "large cap" stocks.

Types of Orders

In order to buy or sell an investment you are going to have to submit an order to your brokerage. This order will stipulate both the price at which you are willing to trade and the timeframe you are willing to have this trade take place. Let's start with the two basic orders based on price.

Market Orders

This is an order that is immediately executed once you submit it. Be careful with these types of orders because as they are filled immediately, there are no limits or restrictions on its execution. A sell order is executed at the current highest bid price and a buy order is executed at the lowest offering price available. You might not necessarily know what the current available pricing is that will match up with your market order so proceed with caution. I knew a person who once put in a market order to sell 500 shares of a stock that was currently trading at $1.00 per share and it sold immediately to someone who had an order to buy 500 shares of the same stock at $.21 per share. The transaction was completed within minutes leaving one customer very happy and one incredibly miserable.

Limit Orders

An order of this type limits the acceptable sale or purchase price to be no less or more than the price you have set. In other words, my friend should have placed a limit order on the 500 shares of stock he was trying to sell at about $1.00 per share. This guarantees the order will only be filled when someone is willing to spend no less than $1.00 per share. On the other side of this scenario, someone had placed a limit order to buy 500 shares of that same stock for $.21 per share.

This guaranteed him that the order would not be filled for more than $.21 per share. The market order guarantees first that the order gets filled and the price is secondary.

Orders Based on Time

Each order you place will have to first explain the pricing you desire and second dictate the timeframe you wish to have it filled. There are several types but these are the ones you will see and use most often.

- **Day** – This order will expire when the market closes at the end of the day if it has not already been filled.
- **Good Till Canceled** – This order will not expire until it is filled or cancelled.
- **Fill Or Kill** – These types of orders must be filled immediately or they will be cancelled.
- **All Or None** – These orders involve multiple shares or units and must be executed in full or not at all. These orders do not have to be filled immediately.

This is a good time to answer a few questions I'm sure you're already asking yourself:

Can the value of your investment decrease? What happens to your money then?

Yes, even if your funds are invested in a money market account, there is still no guarantee the value of your account will not decrease. But let's get something straight here, you don't lose money on an investment until you sell! Yes, too many people fall victim to the "buy high, sell low" strategy. Most commonly, this scenario involves the following steps:

1. You buy into an investment,
2. the price decreases,
3. you panic, and then,
4. you sell the investment thus locking in that loss.

How many times have you pulled the plug on an investment only to watch the price sail back up the next day? More times than not, I'm sure.

Strategy – my investment is doing well, should I "let it ride?"

Your choice, but you never lose when you take the profit. I repeat, **YOU NEVER LOSE WHEN YOU TAKE A PROFIT.** The opposite can happen here compared to the problem discussed above. The following scenario plays out in these steps:

1. You buy into an investment,
2. the price increases,
3. the price increases again,
4. you wonder how high the price will go,
5. you sell at your original purchase price to avoid the earlier scenario. More on this later.

What if there was a way to capitalize on short, quick movements in a stock's price change?

What if you could profit from a stock's price going up OR down?

What if you incorporated a simple strategy that could multiply your account value so you could reach your goals sooner?

What if you gave yourself options in your investment portfolio?

Chapter 2
<u>Options</u>

What the heck is an option?

Simply put, an option is a contract. This contract obligates the holder to purchase (or sell) equities in a company at a future date for a certain price. Most of the time, these equities are shares of stock in that given company. Later on, if you want to go off on your own and experiment with trading contracts in commodities such as oil, chicken eggs, and gold, be my guest. For the time being, we are going to stick with options contracts based on the company's underlying stock.

There are two basic types of option contracts:

Calls and Puts.

Call Options are the right to buy stock for a particular price by a chosen expiration date. Imagine having the ability to buy 100 gallons of gasoline for $3.50 a gallon six months from now. How would you feel if the market price for gasoline exceeded $4.00 a gallon six months from now? It's the same thing with stocks. You are promising to buy stocks in the near future for a certain price which you think will seem like a bargain later. In essence, you are betting on the price of a stock to increase in value.

Put Options are the right to sell stock for a particular price by a chosen expiration date. This is the opposite of the Call Option.

Put Options tend to be a little confusing until you get used to the idea. Here, you are basically betting on the price of a stock to decrease in value. Let's use the gasoline example again. Gas prices are at $4.00 a gallon and you think price will be going down in the near future. So you propose a contract (Put Option) that says you are willing to sell 100 gallons of gas six months from now for $3.80 a gallon. How would you feel if gas prices went down to $3.50 a gallon six months from now?

Every transaction has to have a purchase and a sale, but they don't necessarily have to be in that order. What's actually happening when you exercise a Put Option is that you are first selling borrowed shares of stock in the open market while simultaneously buying shares of the same stock. Hopefully you buy at a lower price than you already sold for. This is how Billy Ray and his friends get rich while making the bad guys poor in the movie, "Trading Places."

OK – basic things to know about all options:

- Each contract covers 100 shares of stock
- The cost of purchasing the option contract is called the premium.
- The price at which the contract owner is entitled to buy or sell the underlying stock is called the exercise or strike price.
- Option contracts expire on the third Friday of the chosen month of your contract.

How do we read an option quote? Here's an example:

XYZ May 60 Call 1.50

Easy, this example is showing us 1 Call Option Contract for XYZ Company. The Strike Price is $60 per share and the contract expires on the third Friday of May. The market price for this contract is listed at $1.50. Remember, each contract represents a block of 100 shares of the underlying stock so it will cost you $150.00 to purchase this option.

You've done your research and you see that XYZ stock shares are trading at $55 per share and May is five months away. By purchasing this particular contract you are actually purchasing the RIGHT to purchase 100 shares of XYZ stock at $60 per share by May.

So you've jumped in and purchased the option contract at $1.50. That's a $150 investment. It's only January so we have some time before this contract needs to be exercised. I'll mention here that there will be fees your brokerage firm will charge on each transaction. But we won't figure those fees into the numbers just to keep the math simple.

Over a few weeks we notice shares of XYZ Company stock are trading at $65 per share. OK, now we're talking. We could exercise this contract because we have the right to buy 100 shares of XYZ Company stock at $60 a share which means we're already in the profit, or "in the money" by $5 per share. Or, we check to see what the value of the options contract is worth at this time and we see that the going rate for this particular contract is $2.50. This is just an example, actual results will vary.

Some other investor out there would just love to have the option of buying a chunk of $65 stock at $60. So, we could sell our option at the new market rate and pocket $1.00 profit. Remember, we're dealing in terms of 100 so that means selling the contract for $250 and keeping a $100 profit !!

Had you purchased 2 of these options, you could have pocketed $200 !!

That's a 67% return on this investment. Did your CD get that kind of return last year? How about over the last 10 years?

Yes there's a distinct and real possibility that this investment could have resulted in a loss. Let's say XYZ Company's stock price hovers and stays at $55 per share. We're not "in the money" and no one seems to be speculating that the price will reach $60 per share by May. So the price of the contract may hover and remain at $50 per share. Quite possibly this option contract may be trading at approximately $.50. That's 50 cents! This means you are $100 down in the value of this investment. Remember, you don't actually realize a loss until you sell out of the investment. So, you could hang on to it and hope the price goes back up or sell to keep what little is left in it.

Fun, huh?

Unlike roulette, you need to do everything you can to keep the odds in your favor. NO, you are not going to hit every time. But if you could earn a modest return MOST of the time you could slowly turn a small savings into the nest egg of your dreams.

You don't always have to pick a winner. There is money to be made in loser companies as well. Yes, I'm talking about using Put Options as part of your investing strategy. These work exactly like the Call Options – just in reverse!

Let's look at this example:

XYZ   May   60   Put   1.50

We already know how to read this. This example is showing us 1 Put Option Contract for XYZ Company. The Strike Price is $60 per share and the contract expires on the third Friday of May. The market price for this contract is listed at $1.50. Remember, each contract represents a block of 100 shares of the underlying stock so it will cost you $150.00 (plus transaction fees) to purchase this option.

Same as the Call Option! Only this time we're really betting that the stock price will DECREASE to $60 per share or lower. In our earlier scenario XYZ Company stock was trading at $55 per share and we were speculating the price would rise to $60 per share or higher. This time, let's say that this stock is currently trading at $65 per share. Your research is suggesting that XYZ Company business hasn't been that great and you expect the stock price to be effected. Normally this might not be a stock that you'd want to purchase outright because smart investors want to buy low and sell high. So why would you invest in a company with a sluggish forecast?

Because by trading with Options we can make money if a stock goes up OR down! Much like the earlier scenario with the Call Option, you've jumped in and purchased this Put Option contract at $1.50. That's a $150 investment. It's still only January and the stock is currently trading at $65 per share so we have some time before this contract needs to be exercised.

Over a few weeks we notice shares of XYZ Company stock are trading lower at $55 per share. We could exercise this contract right now because we have the right to buy 100 shares of XYZ Company stock at $60 a share which means we're now in the profit, or "in the money" by $5 per share. Or, we check to see what the value of the options contract is worth at this time and we see that the going rate for this particular contract is $2.50.

Some other investor out there would just love to have the option of buying a chunk of $60 stock at $55. So, we could sell our option at the new market rate and pocket $1.00 profit. Remember, we're dealing in terms of 100 so that means selling the contract for $250 and keeping a $100 profit.

Yes, there is still a real possibility that investing in a Put Option could result in a loss. Just as we saw in the Call Option scenario, if the XYZ stock price moves in the opposite direction we are expecting it to move, we lose money. So, if we have a Put Option on XYZ company and the stock price increases in value, we lose money.

Options for Wealth, c. 2011, http://optionsforwealth.weebly.com, Brian.Archer.13@gmail.com

How are options valued?

The market value of each options contract is completely based on what investors are willing to pay for these investments. This price per contract is not set by the underlying security it represents and trades independently based on its own market forces. For instance, shares of XYZ Company stock may be trading at $60 per share while the going rate for **XYZ May 60 Put** may be $1.00.

It's possible that shares of XYZ Company stock may start trading higher with no effect on the market value of this option contract. Conversely, XYZ Company stock may be trading with no change in value but this option contract may increase or decrease in value.

What will cause the value of your option contract to fluctuate?

Lots of things. But mostly investor speculation that the price of the underlying stock it represents will change in value. We may see small changes in a stock price in the correct direction but investors still may not have enough confidence this is a strong enough trend. I recommend patience in this case.

What's also going to greatly affect the price of an option is how much demand exists for that option. Just like stocks, if more investors are looking for a XYZ May 60 Call, the price could very well increase. If no one really wants it, the low demand could cause the price to sink.

* CAUTION *

One factor MUST be kept in mind when trading options as it can have a HUGE impact on the value of an options contract. This is called **TIME DECAY**.

As an options contract moves closer to the expiration date, the profitability DECREASES.   For example, the closer we get to the expiration date of a contract the easier it gets to predict where the stock price will be by that day.   The value of the option will decrease exponentially! This means it will have little effect on the value of the option at the beginning, but once we get within 30-40 days of the expiration date the value will drop DRAMATICALLY !!

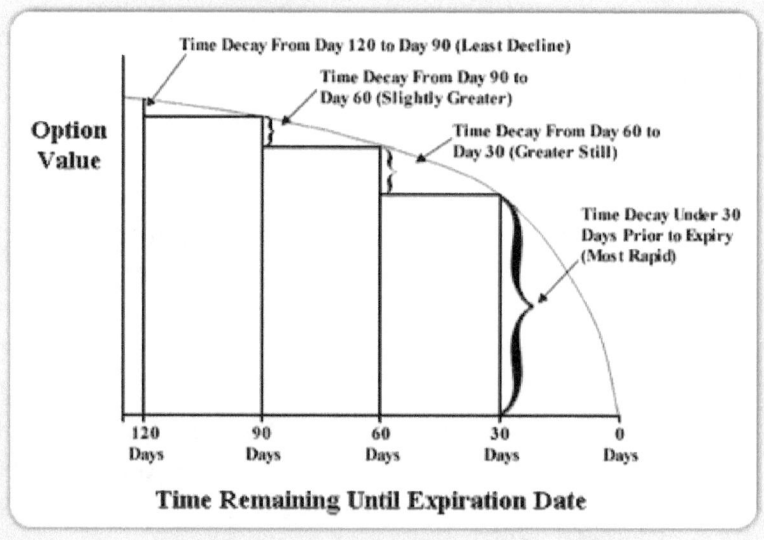

* http://www.timemeansmoney.com/options-time-decay.htm

Scary, huh?

This may be the biggest reason for having a developed investment strategy before jumping into the investment game. The first rule of thumb I like to use – don't buy into an investment until you know **EXACTLY WHAT YOU'RE EXIT STRATEGY IS.** The second rule is – **STICK TO THE PLAN.**

I know this guy who hit big on a slot machine on one particular trip to Las Vegas. Over $1,500 fell into his lap (literally) on one of his first pulls. He chose to keep half and continue to gamble with the other half. Sounds like a good strategy, right? Gamble the house's money, not yours. So, my two cardinal investing rules break out like this:

Rule #1 – The exit strategy was to keep half of the winnings as guaranteed profit.

Rule #2 – Keep half of the winnings as guaranteed profit.

Again, you don't lose when you walk away with a profit. You guessed it, he forgot Rule #2 and didn't stick to the plan. He gambled away the house's money in his pocket then proceeded to "dip" into his winnings a little at a time until that was all gone. And, to make matters even worse, he REPEATEDLY ran to the ATM to pull out even more money out of his checking account (joint account with his wife, mind you) with the idea that he could hit again in order to break even.

Brilliant, eh?

That's why I suggest setting a comfortable goal for getting in and getting out. When you're unsure of yourself and where this investment may be going, pull out and see what you can learn from this experience. Would you pay a few dollars in order to learn a valuable lesson for later? So walk away from it and assess what you can learn for next time.

10% might be a sound goal. This is just a suggestion. If you buy into a Call Option with a premium of $1.00 and the value increases to $1.10, you've just earned 10% on your money. Ten percent! What are CDs paying these days, 2% annually? Do you think you could earn 10% on your money once a month and grow your nest egg? Definitely possible.

10% a month could also mean several investments adding up to your goal of 10% growth for the month. For example, Investment #1 nets you 3%, Investment #2 nets you 7%, and Investment #3 nets you 0%. You didn't score your goal on one investment play but it still adds up to your 10% goal – you win !!

Let it ride

When you start investing based on emotion, you are not stacking the odds in your favor. You will not be in control, you will lose, you will be sad. Don't mistake luck as a sign that you're an investing guru. Once the target price is reached, too many people wait to see how it might grow, undoubtedly screaming "let it ride."

But no one will tell you ahead of time, "this stock's value will tank tomorrow and you better sell now."

Shoulda, woulda, coulda. In competitive shooting terms, when your target is in sight, pull the trigger.

So easy a kid can do it.

Unlike this kid, we probably need to know what we're aiming at. Let's look as some sample goal setting and strategy.

Chapter 3
<u>Personal Goals</u>

So, how would you like to tell people that your retirement account is growing at 10% a month with no risk? Too good to be true? The best way to grow your account by 10% a month is to simply deposit the equivalent of 10% of the account value each month. There you go, risk free account growth. You are on your way to a million in the bank.

Get yourself out of the gate and in the race

10% monthly growth sounds amazing considering how people love to boast how they found a CD paying 4% interest over an entire year. But look at this chart below. That 10% doesn't look too scary, does it?

Could you throw into your account 10, 11, 12, 13, etc dollars each month according to this schedule? Yes you can. Get in the habit of trying to reach that monthly savings goal. The longer you can keep up with the deposit goal, the longer your account will grow 10% a month risk-free.

This chart on the following page shows how an initial $100 can grow 285% over the course of 12 months and 895% over 24 months.

Month	Mthly Goal	Balance	Month	Mthly Goal	Balance
1	$0	$100	25	$90	$985
2	10	110	26	98	1,083
3	11	121	27	108	1,192
4	12	133	28	119	1,311
5	13	146	29	131	1,442
6	15	161	30	144	1,586
7	16	177	31	159	1,745
8	18	195	32	174	1,919
9	19	214	33	192	2,111
10	21	236	34	211	2,323
11	24	259	35	232	2,555
12	26	285	36	255	2,810
13	29	314	37	281	3,091
14	31	345	38	309	3,400
15	35	380	39	340	3,740
16	38	418	40	374	4,114
17	42	459	41	411	4,526
18	46	505	42	453	4,979
19	51	556	43	498	5,476
20	56	612	44	548	6,024
21	61	673	45	602	6,626
22	67	740	46	663	7,289
23	74	814	47	729	8,018
24	81	895	48	802	8,820

For those of you that are more graphically disposed, this is next chart shows what your account growth will look like if it followed the 10% monthly growth pattern.

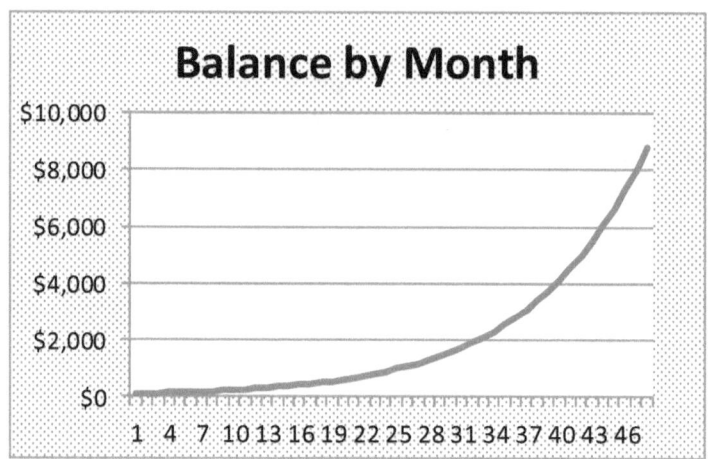

This looks like a pretty good start. At some point you will have already incorporated investing in some options contracts. I recommend having approximately $500 in the account before making actual trades. This is to allow you the flexibility to afford a wider variety of options. Some contracts will require an investment around $40 but some contracts can be priced well over $300. It stinks when you see an opportunity that you just can't afford. I have made the mistake (which I will talk about later) of trying to purchase a lower-priced contract that didn't pan out as well as the higher-priced contracts. The important first step is to get the account funded. Now you're ready to leap into action.

Take Action #1: Put money in your account. Anything. Whatever change is in your pocket right now.

Take Action #2: Research 3 good companies

These will be the companies you will trade regularly for the long-term so get comfortable with them. You want to know as much about them as possible like stock price history, any seasonal patterns, does the stock trade with significant volume.   Regular volume is necessary so you know you have a good chance of buying or selling an option when you want to instead of waiting for long periods of time (sometimes days) for your transaction to go through.   You also run a greater risk of not getting your desired price when the transaction finally goes through.

Here are some online research tools I like to use. There are many others but these are free and will get you started:

www.bigcharts.marketwatch.com/

www.FeeStockCharts.com

www.clearstation.etrade.com/

www.Interactivebrokers.com

www.bloomberg.com/

www.ChartPattern.com

www.stockcharts.com/

www.StockCharts.com

www.dailyfinance.com/stock-charts/

www.Working-Money.com

www.finance.yahoo.com/

www.Traders.com

Take Action #3: Paper Trade

While you're researching your companies, watch how their price has fluctuated historically. Learn how much movement is required of the stock price to net your goal profit. Try out (on paper) some practice trades based on past stock price information and then on current data.

Try this:

1. Pick a company. Any company really but maybe one you are really hot for trying some options on.
2. Find the company's option charts from one of your research websites.

3. Find the charts for options expiring approximately six months from now.

4. Find the prices on both the Call Option and the Put Option that are just in and just out of the money. Here's an example:

	CALLS					PUTS				
Last	Change	Vol.	Bid	Ask	Strike Price	Last	Change	Vol.	Bid	Ask
0.17	-0.03	18,222.00	0.17	0.19	**27.00**	0.18	-0.03	8,030.00	0.16	0.18
		Current Stock Price			**27.42**					
0.02		1,530.00	0.01	0.02	**28.00**	1.04	-0.01	5,527.00	1.00	1.01

5. Write down the "last" price for each of these four contracts. This represents the market price for the Call and Put Option contracts right next to the current Strike Price.

6. Return to this screen on a daily basis to see how the change in the current Stock Price affects the prices of each of these contracts.

Same Option 3 Months Later

	CALLS					PUTS				
Last	Change	Vol.	Bid	Ask	Strike Price	Last	Change	Vol.	Bid	Ask
0.86		2,330	0.82	0.85	**26.00**	0.84		2,615	0.85	0.87
		Current Stock Price			**26.07**					
0.40		1,393	0.40	0.42	**27.00**	1.43		153	1.45	1.48

Review the results. Now you have a great idea how a fluctuating Stock Price affects could affect one of your investments. Don't forget to also factor in the brokerage fees. There is usually a transaction fee for the purchase and the sale of an investment. Given this scenario, would you have purchased a Call or Put option? In or out of the money? Were you right? How much did you gain/lose? You may want to try this exercise with several companies before you start using real dollars.

Take Action #4: Grow your account by 10% each month. Commit to reaching that monthly goal each and every month. That may mean making a small deposit to reach that next level on your growth chart. Be disciplined! Some months will be hard, some months will be easy. If you can, try to stay ahead of your plan.

Chapter 4
Further investing strategy

Traditional Brokerage Account

These types of accounts allow you to buy and sell stocks, bonds, mutual funds, options and other investments. Your contributions are made with after-tax dollars and, depending on the financial institution, usually don't have any maximums. There may be a minimum initial deposit however. Transactions and earnings within the account have tax implications so be careful and consult a professional before, during, and after setting up such an account.

Individual Retirement Account (IRA)

This is a retirement account that can provide some tax advantages generally for retirement savings. This account is generally set up for an individual but it can be set up as a joint account or as a trust or custodial account. As of 2011, the contribution limit per individual is $5,000. These contributions are made with after-tax dollars but may be deducted from your annual taxes. All transactions and earnings within the account have no tax impact. Withdrawals however are taxed as income. Any withdrawals made before age 59 ½ are subject to early withdrawal tax penalties (usually an additional 10%).

Many people hold the misconception that an IRA is merely a repository for retirement money and nothing else. That it is just like a "savings account." That's partially true. Yes, think of the IRA as the shell account but the inside can be whatever you want it to be. A friend of mine has an insurance policy set up as the lone investment within an IRA. Your IRA could be merely a sole money market savings account. A brokerage account makes a very acceptable IRA.

For those of you who have an educational goal for their kids and/or loved ones, an IRA can serve as a useful planning tool to reach those financial needs. Obviously by taking a distribution from your IRA you are reducing the pile of cash (nest egg) you would otherwise use to spend your golden years. Any distribution taken from this account would also be considered taxable income for that calendar year. However, distributions can be made **penalty-free** in cases where the proceeds are used to pay **higher education costs, a first-time home purchase, or medical premiums among others.**

Roth IRA

Similar to the Traditional IRA, contributions are made with after-tax dollars to a limit of $5,000 per year. Also, all transactions and earnings within the account have no tax impact. Any withdrawals made before age 59 ½ are subject to early withdrawal tax penalties.

However, withdrawals from these accounts are not taxed as income. This means you can have tax-free income in your golden years.

Also, if you were looking to use funds from this account to help pay for higher education, the same rules apply as they did with the traditional IRA. If you take a distribution from a Roth IRA before age 59 ½ you will also incur a 10% tax penalty on the amount of the withdrawal. As long as the withdrawal is used as discussed above, no penalties will apply.

To sum up, a Roth IRA allows you to grow your money tax-free and in certain circumstances, you may withdrawal that tax-free money without penalties. To fully understand the tax advantages of the Roth IRA you should consult your personal financial advisor or accountant. But this is what I see as the best scenario for many people. Inside the Roth IRA you can trade Call and Put Options and grow your nest egg tax deferred and quite possibly set yourself up with tax-free income in your golden years.

401(k) Plan

This is a tax-deferred retirement plan offered and sponsored by an employer. These plans allow you to set money away each paycheck, before taxes, into an account from which you can draw from once you hit retirement. The funds also grow tax exempt like the IRA. Withdrawals however are taxed as income. Any withdrawals made before age 59 ½ are subject to early withdrawal tax penalties.

Generally the employer will contribute an amount to your account if you participate. **This is free money – TAKE IT!!** Contribute at least as much as your employer is willing to contribute

Most of these plans only carry a handful of investment choices within the account. An individual participant usually has a choice of a money market account and several mutual funds. Usually you can diversify the portfolio by having a portion of your money deposited into one, several, or all of the available investments. Also, depending upon the plan, you can periodically transfer money between these investments.

403(b) Plan

This is a tax-deferred retirement plan, much like the 401(k), offered and sponsored by public sector and non-profit employers. The structure of these accounts are similar to that of 401(k) plans.

Chapter 5
<u>Final Motivation</u>

I made this mistake once where I couldn't afford the Call Option I wanted so I bought a different option I could afford. My thought was that I could earn the same percentage profit, just on a smaller scale. Wrong! Here's the story – there was this energy stock hovering in the low $60's per share and my research told me it would trade in the $90's in a few months. Now, the option I wanted was a Call Option, 5 months out, with a strike price of $65. The premium for this option was currently trading at $3.50 but I only had about $100 in available cash. I was afraid of losing the opportunity of this stock's upward mobility so I made the impulsive move of purchasing the Call Option I could afford. This Option had an expiration of 5 months out as well with a strike price of $100. The premium for this Option was $.90.

The stock moved up in value just as my research said it would, rising above $80 in 3 weeks. The Option I originally wanted increased in value to $6.50 while the option I actually purchased rose to a stunning $1.03. That's when I sold out of the investment, took my 10% and called it a win.

My point here is that I made an investment decision to force a purchase because I was scared of missing an opportunity. The option I purchased took a while before it moved at all and for a while I thought it was going to lose me money. I sweated over this one and was relieved to get out of it in the positive. The moral here is that buying an Option and praying it will work out is NOT an investment strategy !

Let's face it. We're all a little lazy. If it's too complicated, we're going to look for another way. If we're looking for a car and we find a one that will need some TLC, we're probably going to pass on it in order to look for something with fewer issues. Some of us actually like extra drama in our lives but most of us don't.

A lot of people go about planning that nest egg for retirement the same way they go about diets and weight-loss. They buy a book that promises the solid, no way you can lose method for making all your dreams come true. But once they open the book, it's like a deer in the headlights. They get super-stimulated, can't focus, panic sets in, anxiety takes over, and guess what? People fall back to what's familiar.

The military understands this concept all too well. That's the point of basic training – to create a fundamental baseline from which every soldier can "fall back" to. In the heat of battle, when a soldier is faced with a challenging situation (the Air Force calls this a sand trap), they have learned to fall back to what they learned in training.

Money has been around about as long as people have walked the earth. And we have sought it equally as hard as we have sought partnership with a life-mate. You could say our relationship with money is similar to our relationships with significant others. Money has broken our hearts and made us feel whole. Some say money can't buy happiness but some count on money to buy happiness, maybe even love. Some people count on money for peace of mind. One thing is for certain, money means exactly something different to each and every one of us. So find your inspiration and write down your goals.

Here's what some people had to say:

The only reason a great many American families don't own an elephant is that they have never been offered an elephant for a dollar down and easy weekly payments. *~ Mad Magazine*

I'd like to live as a poor man with lots of money. *~ Pablo Picasso*

Money is better than poverty, if only for financial reasons.
~ Woody Allen

Money can't buy happiness, but it can buy you the kind of misery you prefer. ~ *Author Unknown*

Money is power, freedom, a cushion, the root of all evil, the sum of blessings. ~ *Carl Sandburg*

I've been rich and I've been poor: Rich is better. ~ *Sophie Tucker*

Lack of money is the root of all evil. *~ George Bernard Shaw*

A dollar picked up in the road is more satisfaction to us than the 99 which we had to work for, and the money won at Faro or in the stock market snuggles into our hearts in the same way.
~ Mark Twain

A nickel ain't worth a dime anymore. *~ Yogi Berra*

If you want to succeed you should strike out on new paths, rather than travel the worn paths of accepted success.
~ *John D. Rockefeller*

Discover your goals
Find your rhythm
Fall back to this book.
Keep it simple.
Start your account today.
Start it with a buddy.
Start it with the whole family.

Whether you ride a roller coaster or merry-go-round,
Have fun with it.

Brian Archer, MPA

With more than 20 years of diverse business experience, Brian has developed an eclectic range of expertise. As a former Air Force Officer formally trained in Aerospace Engineering, he gained extensive experience planning, developing, and leading large teams through multi-million dollar government technology development programs for the US and foreign governments.

Advanced studies came in the field of Public Policy and Urban Planning. He has consulted with various government, public and not-for-profit organizations to model and redevelop work process enhancements primarily in the development of commercial and multi-zone development projects.

Brian earned his Series 7, 63, and Insurance licensing many moons ago and has passionately served the clients that most needed his skills – those that could least afford a professional.

Reference

Companies Comprising the Dow Jones Industrial Average

Company	Symbol	Industry
3M	MMM	Conglomerate
Alcoa	AA	Aluminum
American Express	AXP	Consumer Finance
AT&T	T	Telecommunication
Bank of America	BAC	Banking
Boeing	BA	Aerospace & Defense
Caterpillar	CAT	Const. & Mining Equip.
Chevron Corp	CVX	Oil & Gas
Cisco	CSCO	Computer Networking
Coca-Cola	KO	Beverages
DuPont	DD	Chemicals
ExxonMobil	XOM	Oil and Gas
General Electric	GE	Conglomerate
Hewlett-Packard	HPQ	Technology
The Home Depot	HD	Retail
Intel	INTC	Technology
IBM	IBM	Technology
Johnson & Johnson	JNJ	Pharmaceuticals
JP Morgan Chase	JPM	Banking
Kraft Foods	KFT	Food Processing
McDonald's	MCD	Food Retail
Merck	MRK	Pharmaceuticals
Microsoft	MSFT	Technology
Pfizer	PFE	Pharmaceuticals
Procter & Gamble	PG	Consumer Goods
Travelers	TRV	Insurance
United Technologies Corp	UTX	Conglomerate
Verizon Communications	VZ	Telecommunications
Wal-Mart	WMT	Retail
Walt Disney	DIS	Broadcasting & Ent.

Dow Jones Industrial Average 1900 – 2011

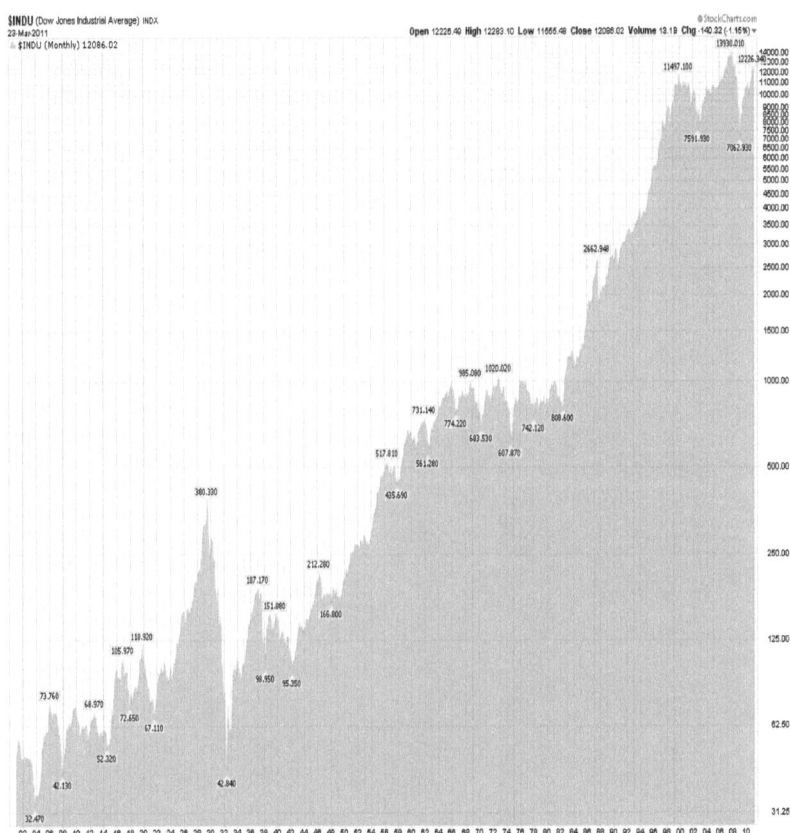

* http://stockcharts.com/charts/historical/djia1900.html

Russell 2000 Index 1987 -2011

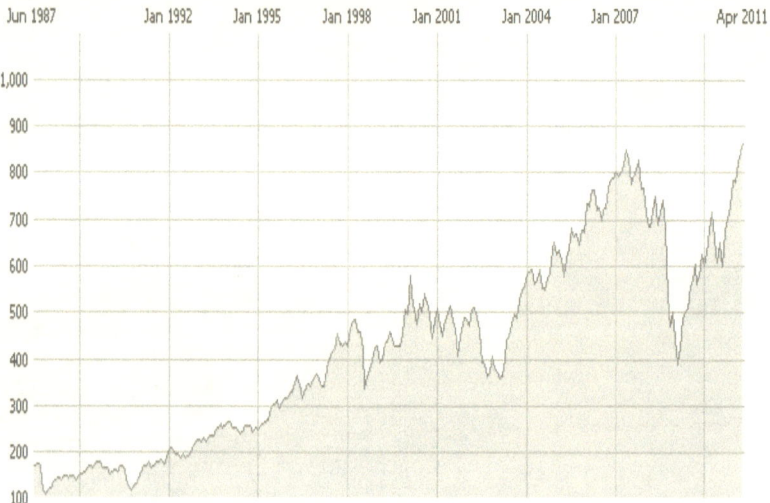

Standard & Poors 500 Index 1960 - 2011

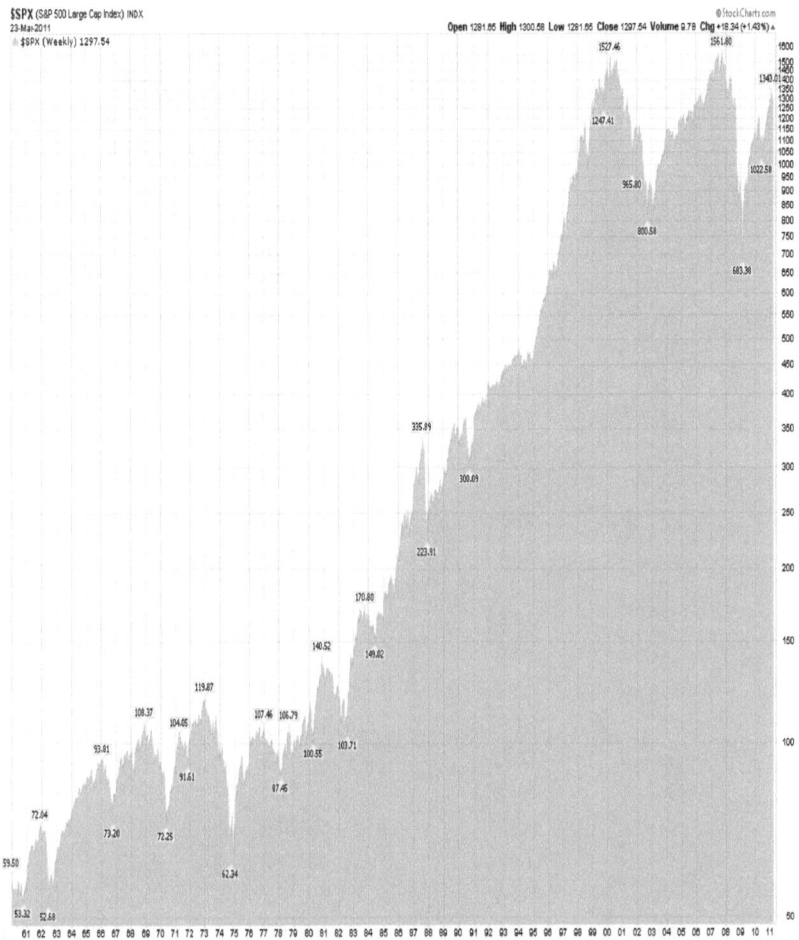

Account Balance Accrual at 10% Monthly

Month	Mthly Goal	Balance	Month	Mthly Goal	Balance
1	$0	$100	25	$90	$985
2	10	110	26	98	1,083
3	11	121	27	108	1,192
4	12	133	28	119	1,311
5	13	146	29	131	1,442
6	15	161	30	144	1,586
7	16	177	31	159	1,745
8	18	195	32	174	1,919
9	19	214	33	192	2,111
10	21	236	34	211	2,323
11	24	259	35	232	2,555
12	26	285	36	255	2,810
13	29	314	37	281	3,091
14	31	345	38	309	3,400
15	35	380	39	340	3,740
16	38	418	40	374	4,114
17	42	459	41	411	4,526
18	46	505	42	453	4,979
19	51	556	43	498	5,476
20	56	612	44	548	6,024
21	61	673	45	602	6,626
22	67	740	46	663	7,289
23	74	814	47	729	8,018
24	81	895	48	802	8,820

Account Balance Accrual at 10% Monthly (cont'd)

Month	Mthly Goal	Balance		Month	Mthly Goal	Balance
49	$882	$9,702		85	$27,264	$299,906
50	970	10,672		86	29,991	329,897
51	1,067	11,739		87	32,990	362,887
52	1,174	12,913		88	36,289	399,175
53	1,291	14,204		89	39,918	439,093
54	1,420	15,625		90	43,909	483,002
55	1,562	17,187		91	48,300	531,302
56	1,719	18,906		92	53,130	584,432
57	1,891	20,797		93	58,443	642,876
58	2,080	22,876		94	64,288	707,163
59	2,288	25,164		95	70,716	777,880
60	2,516	27,680		96	77,788	855,668
61	2,768	30,448		97	85,567	941,234
62	3,045	33,493		98	94,123	1,035,358
63	3,349	36,842		99	103,536	1,138,894
64	3,684	40,527		100	113,889	1,252,783
65	4,053	44,579		101	125,278	1,378,061
66	4,458	49,037		102	137,806	1,515,867
67	4,904	53,941		103	151,587	1,667,454
68	5,394	59,335		104	166,745	1,834,200
69	5,933	65,268		105	183,420	2,017,619
70	6,527	71,795		106	201,762	2,219,381
71	7,180	78,975		107	221,938	2,441,320
72	7,897	86,872		108	244,132	2,685,451
73	8,687	95,559		109	268,545	2,953,997
74	9,556	105,115		110	295,400	3,249,396
75	10,512	115,627		111	324,940	3,574,336
76	11,563	127,190		112	357,434	3,931,770
77	12,719	139,908		113	393,177	4,324,946
78	13,991	153,899		114	432,495	4,757,441
79	15,390	169,289		115	475,744	5,233,185
80	16,929	186,218		116	523,319	5,756,504
81	18,622	204,840		117	575,650	6,332,154
82	20,484	225,324		118	633,215	6,965,370
83	22,532	247,856		119	696,537	7,661,907
84	24,786	272,642		120	766,191	8,428,097

Options for Wealth, c. 2011, http://optionsforwealth.weebly.com, Brian.Archer.13@gmail.com

- NOTES -

- NOTES -

- NOTES -